Southern Reflections with a
little help from my friends

Madalyn McKnight Stanford

AuthorHouse™
1663 Liberty Drive, Suite 200
Bloomington, IN 47403
www.authorhouse.com
Phone: 1-800-839-8640

AuthorHouse™ UK Ltd.
500 Avebury Boulevard
Central Milton Keynes, MK9 2BE
www.authorhouse.co.uk
Phone: 08001974150

First published by AuthorHouse 12/13/2006

ISBN: 978-1-4259-7180-9 (sc)

Printed in the United States of America
Bloomington, Indiana

This book is printed on acid-free paper.

Bloomington, IN Milton Keynes, UK

authorHOUSE®

Dedicated: to all the children in my life
whom I consider "Grand."

Hannah
Amanda
Katherine
Kristian
Matthew
John
Andrew
James
Garrett
Austin

Foreword by Forrest Laws

If you spend much time with a person who is visually impaired, you soon learn that he or she can bring an added dimension to your life. Trying to describe a flower or a sunset or simply warning them about an obstacle forces you to look at things on a deeper plane and to choose your words carefully. As the daughter of a father who lost his sight in his early twenties, Madalyn McKnight Stanford grew up choosing her words to convey images her father could no longer see.

Bob McKnight was never bitter about his loss. He taught himself to play five musical instruments and led a band that performed on radio. He became a public servant, opening the first state Office of Rehabilitation in Memphis, Tennessee, and running it under five presidents. He told his daughter he saw the world through her eyes and wanted vivid descriptions of things and colors. As she grew older, Madalyn read to her father and those sessions turned into lively debates about the books and about their world.

Madalyn's world was not atypical. She grew up as a city girl in Memphis, but, like many city residents who spent their formative years in the 1950s and 60s, she became "bilingual." That is, her frequent visits with grandparents, aunts, uncles and cousins made her just as much at home in rural Mississippi as on the streets of the city. You don't have to read far into *Southern Reflections* to see the depth of feeling those memories hold.

But this is more than a book about reminiscences. Underneath the folksy humor and sometimes irreverent language is an edge - a longing not only for what used to be but also for what might have been. It's as if she has peeled back the veneer and invited her readers to take a deeper look at her life and life in the rural South and Memphis and at the family she shares with her husband, Jim. Bob McKnight is probably looking down and smiling.

Forrest Laws is executive editor at *Delta Farm Press* a weekly farm newspaper in the Mid-South. A native of Arkansas, he received his bachelor's and master's degrees from The University of Memphis. He was a police reporter and business writer for the now-defunct *Memphis Press-Scimitar.* He joined Farm Press Publications in 1980. Besides writing a weekly column on legislative and environmental issues, he has written extensively on farm marketing, production practices and new technology. He has also authored two books on conservation tillage farming. He and his wife, Colleen, have two children and three grandchildren

Thank You

To my friend, great actor, artist and cartoonist, Jim Palmer
of Memphis, TN., who designed the perfect cover for this work.

To my strength of mind and weakness of heart, my husband Dr. Jim Stanford.

To my children, their spouses and my grand children who keep me
laughing and make life interesting.

To my pastor, mentor and friend, Dr. Brent Beasley.

To my friends in community theatre for sharing their lives and
stories with me.

To the Messick High School Class of 1959 for being my friends
for so long.

THANK YOU ALL

As a child I was continually reminded by loving parents that, "you are what you eat, you are what you read and you are the company you keep." I have not always eaten the right things but, I've read everything I could get my hands on. The last admonition was the best by far. The company I've kept over the years, my friends, make me look far better than I would if left to my own devices.

I owe a great deal to the line of strong women from which I came. There was an educated Grandmother who came to a small rural community to teach school and married the son of her host family, farmed and raised a large family on extremely meager wages and subsistence. A Grandmother who kept her own house and ran a florist to which she had to ride a bus to and from work until she was 84 years old. Then there is also the adventurous Mother who left her rural upbringing and moved 200 miles north to the big city, as a very young girl, to marry a blind musician, with a son by a previous marriage. There are those women who took up arms to defend their homes during Civil wars, although they believed there was nothing civil about any war. They always did what they had to do.

Madalyn McKnight Stanford

Table of Contents

Remnant

Silent sentinel standing alone
Monument to life too soon gone.
Born in that house, died there too
In the way a person shouldn't do.
Family raised in country air
Scattered now everywhere.
He loved working his fields by day.
He prayed and sang as was his way.
To read the Bible was his delight.
He kept it open both day and night.
His needs were small, a stove, a chair,
A single bed, they found him there.
A furtive stranger entered alone
Destroyed the sanctity of his home.
Nothing valuable did he keep
And for that nothing, died in his sleep.
Fugitive nor weapon never found
His bones now rest in cold, cold ground.
This remnant of life now overgrown
Sits cold and empty, all alone.

Escalation To War

Which way the arrow of my care
Its poisoned point took me unaware
The dart was flung with religious force
By friend not enemy, of course

<>======%======<>

Who got so close to know me well
Spurned my secrets all to tell
Of this betrayal, I will not die
Twas ill conceived you sought to lie

<>=============%=============<>

Yours eyes instead your deception told
As they looked into mine fervently bold
I load my arrow, pull back the bow
With fiery words my fury show

<>=================%=================<>

Escalation to war and so it goes
Finding ourselves in hatreds throes
Defiled my name, invaded my space
Retaliation the only way to save face.

<>====================%====================<>

Tsunami

The earth breathed.
Life was in conflict.
Inhaling uncountable gallons of water.
Gasped and exhaled,
belching death in each drop.
Roaring, thrashing, gathering its souvenirs.
Re-depositing them far a field.
Drawn back to its bed.
Tossing murderous reward.
Revealing its plunder.

The Tree Is Me

Bury me not in concrete and steel
But, under a tree on some leaf strewn hill.
Living forever was in the plan
Just not on this earth and not as man.
When did we move so far from the real
Resting in prisons of concrete and steel?
This circle of life has been interrupted
Our return to the soil sorely corrupted.
No marker of stone to show where I passed.
Nurture the earth with something that lasts.
A home for the birds, nectar for the bees
My name whispered by wind in the trees.
By the law of the land I am constrained
From burial on land lawfully obtained.
They want me to rest in cemetery queue
To never, ever rot, mold or even mildew.
So from dust I came as ashes I'll return
But, not confined in some glorified urn.
I care not where my ashes may fall
Part of the life force sustaining us all.

"We are polluting useable land space with objects that will never biodegrade in our lifetime. Destroying the possibility that future generations could use it for food production or other sustaining needs. Why do we seem to have so much trouble letting go when it's such a natural part of life. It is another evidence of selfishness on our part, this wanting to hang on to what is "ours." I would never ask anyone to waste time coming to a cemetery for years after I've moved on and please....if you didn't give me flowers when I could enjoy them... save your money now. Our ancestors built wooden boxes that deteriorated time wise according to the climate of that particular area."

Nearly 200 year old Oak Tree on the family farm in Five Points,
TN. of Hassel Newton, deceased, and Sondra Newton.
A storm in 2005 seriously damaged the wonderful old Oak and necessitated it's removal.
It once was the place up high in it's branches that Hassel, as a child, hid his marbles
and toys from a cousin bent on destroying them. The cousin was afraid to climb.
The lowest limb was so large that it alone held the sister's tree house. It witnessed the Pony
Express Riders in the family and the first Post Office. Only a small portion of the trunk
remains bearing witness to it's former grandeur. When Bobby Brodee was hired to take the
storm ravaged tree down he found the iron bars Hassel had nailed to the tree as his ladder
to reach it's top branches. Sondra still has one of the bars. And the tree is outlined on
Hassel's tombstone in Second Creek Cemetery in Five Points, TN. on the Alabama border.

No Killing Field Today

Lying on the jungle floor mud-caked and wet
Sensed he was out there but, hadn't seen him yet.
He knew I was waiting to get off a shot
I didn't know if I would kill him or not.

I swore allegiance to be the best I could.
I got to my feet and there he stood.
His gun on me and mine on him,
The situation tense, his expression grim.

I broke out in a great big smile.
He did too and we stared a while.
I slowly decided to take a chance
And with heavy boots went into my dance.

First I danced fast, then I danced slower.
He froze at first then his gun barrel lowered.
I leaned over laid my rifle on the ground.
Then he did the same without a sound.

I reached in my pocket and offered him a smoke.
It was then he realized it was no joke
We both sat down on that God forsaken land,
Side by side with a Marlboro in our hands.

Not a word was spoken there was no need.
We just sat silently puffing that weed.
When it was finished he started to stand,
Turned around and gave me his hand.

Once I was upright and on my feet,
There was no way our eyes could not meet.
He gave me a salute and then a nod.
And into the jungle he slowly trod.

War is hell many soldiers say
But, there'll be no killing on this field today.
The story is true, it's not a joke.
Two enemies found peace with a smile and a smoke.

"I am the enemy you killed, my friend.
I knew you in this dark: for so you
frowned Yesterday through me as you
jabbed and killed. I parried; but my
hands were loath and cold.
Let us sleep now..." --
Wilfred Owen, "Strange Meeting",
November 1918

"On body-eating Somme I lay opposite to
you . . . but you didn't know!
Enemy to enemy. Human to human,
body to body, warm and cramped." --
Gefreiter Gerrit Engelke, WWI,
German Soldier

"Comrade, I did not want to kill you. . . .
You were only an idea to me before,
an abstraction that lived in my mind
and called forth its appropriate response.
was that abstraction I stabbed. . . .
Forgive me, comrade. We always see it
too late. Why do they never tell us
that you are poor devils like us,
that your mothers are just as anxious
as ours, and that we have the same fear
of death, and the same dying and the
same agony -- Forgive me, comrade;
how could you be my enemy? If we threw
away these rifles and this uniform you
could be my brother just like Kat. . . ."
-- Erich Maria Remarque,
All Quiet on the Western Front, IX. 195

"The ones who call the shots won't be
among the dead and lame, and on each end
of the rifle we're the same." --
John McCutcheon, "Christmas in the Trenches"

The Baptism

Down into the water they went
Brown women and children all in white.
Their rhythmic chorus heaven sent
Muddy water shining with sunlight.

They all went singing beneath the waves
With smiles on their faces.
I saw only watery graves
They saw only graces.

Standing on the shore
Holding Mama's hand
Straining to see more
Struggled to understand.
Does God want to drown them?
Was the question that I raised.
No child, they're only following him.
Will forever sing his praise.

I too was baptized years later.
In water's clear, this symbol I sought.
God is the great Emancipator.
My freedom his Son's blood bought.

Withdrawal

I'm not I think a misanthrope
Though I like to be alone.

To think and speak from silences.
To value, respect a need for solitude.
Find peace where human voice is not dominant.

I am not lonely when alone,
Regardless of our cultural biases.
My solitary state requires
Neither companionship nor sympathy.

I relish conversation with the universe.

I need to walk alone many more times
Before I'll ever know it's mystery.
If I inhabit this place
I shall, I must reverence
It's silence as well as it's noise.

Bo-Daddy Said at Momma's Funeral

Croaking through dry cracked lips,
don'tcha know how I feel boutcha boy?

Iffin ya don't, I ain't gonna tell ya.
There's just some things in life
you just gotta know.

I ain't talkin bout head knowin.
I mean breath knowin, and smell knowin,
and skin and hair and heart knowin.
Can't count on hearin it.
People don't last, knowin does
and it neva leaves ya.

So, getcha self up now
do whatcha has to do,
and get on with your knowin.

"Elderly African/American Grandfather's advice to his now orphaned grandson at the funeral of
the 9 year olds Mother. Such simple eloquence

My Little Boys

Boys are nasty, smelly, grimey things
with dirty hands and broken shoe strings.
They fight with friend and foe alike.
They tear their clothes and wreck their bikes.

They pull their little sisters hair,
and punch big holes in leather chairs.
They refuse to bathe or brush their teeth.
And hiding dirty clothes under the bed is neat.

Their noses run and they do too
from any work you ask them to do.
They're all grown now, I have no other.
Instead of Mom they call me Mother.

But the party's starting over again.
I Have Male Grandchildren.
AMEN!

We Must Find A Way

*She wrestled all night
in that dark boundary
between
neither here, nor there.
And she was broken
in her indecision.*

Her scars were
twisted, torturous,
angry, red welts that
coursed her naked body
like snakes.

The weapon a long
knotted leather
lead from a
horse's halter

When the decision
was finally made
to extricate herself
and her children,
it was too late.

Her helpless children
watch her as she dangles
from the overhead beam
like a featherless chicken
in the poulterer's window.

And the person who
promised to love and cherish
her is out there
secreting himself
from punishment.

Where is the balm for
the eyes, ears, hearts and minds
of babies only 5 and 7 years old.
Will they ever gain
a sense of awe or wonder
at the miracle of their lives.

Will his demon forever
haunt them?
Will her weakness
soon to be theirs?

So many children,
so much trauma
in lives too young to
understand the madness.

Domestic Abuse
Must Be Stopped!

~

*Opening statement
Paraphrased from sermon
of Dr. Brent Beasley
Second Baptist, Memphis, TN.*

The Stray

A couple snuggling in a dimly lit booth
While the jukebox bumps out Juicy Juice.
The door opens and he walks right in
Gives everyone his big toothy grin.
He strolls right up to a pretty miss.
She holds out her hand and he gives it a kiss.
Goes around the bar and to the back door
To find his dishes still on the floor.
Some kibble and real turkey for a treat
Lots of cold water to help in this heat.
Back to the front he makes his round
Always one step away from the pound.
From where he came no one knows.
Even harder to figure out where he goes.
He wanders in daily with such easy grace
I think, he thinks, he owns this place.

My Editor

I spent all morning composing it.
I taxed my feeble brain.
He found my writing too verbose,
Said I needed to make it plain.
He pulled out a big red marking pen
And began the thankless chore.
He slashed and marked and marked and slashed,
My teenaged son "The Editor."

My spelling was termed atrocious.
My grammar was just insane.
He said he found very little to like,
Even the way I signed my name.
I submitted it to the judges.
I'm not sure that was wise.

They called to say I'd won First Place.
So, I'm giving him the prize.

Conversation With Matthew

Matthew Cole Scoggins

It was the families moving day
late in the afternoon.
We lay on our backs
on the rough scarred planks
of the trailers bottom
and stared into the sky.
I the appointed caregiver
and he my appointed charge.
Quiet easy peace between us.

What are we doin O'ma?

We're being puppies
stretched out on our backs
letting the sun warm
our furry, white bellies.

I see the moon...it's not night.

Sometimes you can see
the moon in the daytime.

Is that bird flying to the moon?

I think he would love
to fly to the moon
but, his wings aren't strong enough
to carry him that far.

I love you, O'ma.

I know.

Can we lay down on the moon
like puppies and let the
sun shine on our bellies?

Yes maybe, one day
but, you can dream about it now.

I know.

And there we lay so close
I can almost feel
that 3 year old heart beating
in my own chest.

I love you , Matthew.

I know.

The Wheelchair Train

There they go, they're doing it again
Trying to escape, their same old plan.
Must be quiet someone will hear.
The pusher is the one in the rear.

Wheelchairs lined up like a train
One pushing, one pulling, they're off again.
Gray hair on top, slippers on their feet
A squirrelly-er pair you'll never meet.

If I had a dollar each time they tried to get away.
I could retire a millionaire today.
They work on the door lock with a hairbrush.
We sit and watch, there's no need to rush.

When the doors are open wide
They never attempt to go outside.
It's the thrill of the game to escape, you see.
They have no real desire to be free.

It keeps their minds fertile, the Nurse said with a smile.
They work all morning, then rest a while.
The afternoon brings the same refrain
Trying to escape in their wheelchair train.

Time Bomb

I carefully charted the course.
Move in from the left
With tool held tightly in hand.
One wrong move and it's all over.

I could feel the vibration starting
Only seconds between me and destruction.
I set to work with precision.
The time was ticking away.

Slowly, gently I made the first sweep
Then another as I knew it was too late.
The explosion rattled my teeth.
I heard myself shrieking.

The red began to spread on the floor.
My last thought, why did I attempt this again?
But No More will I try to...

Polish my toe nails
When I have the hiccups.

Their Brother's Keeper

Eddie Carter and Employees of Midsouth Feed & Seed

He wasn't quite right, his family cried
He disappeared the day his father died
Even the Army kicked him out
Said his emotional stability was in doubt'

He lived under a bridge, near the Feed Store
In a cardboard box, never asking for more
No coat, no socks and toeless shoes
Scavenged trash bins searching for food

He wouldn't take money, he wasn't a bum
No crimes he committed, not on the run
The owner and employees of The Feed Store
Let him sweep up and vowed to do more

They built him a shelter, painted it green
In 20 years the only home he'd seen
A cot and a heater and a warm sleeping bag
Clean clothes finally and disposed of his rags

The woods where his home stood had been sold
He was allowed to stay and his land to hold
A small bath house was built a few steps away
With it's shower and vanity still standing today

On April the fourth in his little green shed
Roy David Randall, age 64 was found dead
The newspaper story told of his fate
His mother, 84 arrived from another state

For years his whereabouts were unknown
She found he had friends, she saw his home.
His ashes were scattered in his beloved woods
While a community that cared prayerfully stood

His friends knew him as a happy man
Always willing to lend you a hand
The minister said we benefited from knowing him
In this world of cut glass...."Roy Randall was a gem."

Fishers of Men

The years were wrapped around her
Like the cloak of many ragged layers she wore
Hobbling behind the rusted grocery cart
And under her breath she swore

<o)))))><

Hair of steel wool an angry mess
Dirt laden bandana piled loosely on top
Socks ridden down halfway into shoes
Account for that crippling hop

<o)))))><

The smell greeted you before she
That putrid, unwashed, old urine smell
What chance of life or roll of dice
Condemned her to this hell

<o)))))><

Why should my soul tremble for her sake
Covered as she was with sores on her skin
The admonition hit like a lightening bolt
Because HE made me a fisher of men.

<o)))))><

Arrangement was made with a small cafe
To provide her a daily meal
The thrift shop on the corner had a thick coat
And was willing to make a deal

<o)))))><

Another store owner had a warm closet
And said she could spend the night
After weeks of some care
In her eyes, we began to see a light

<o)))))><

Now she talks to us freely
The stories she can spin
We sit beside her and listen
We ordinary fishers of men

<o)))))>< <o)))))>< <o)))))><

Too Much Honesty

To Matthew who keeps me humble.

I preened and primped for two hours
Searched my closet for appropriate attire
Generously applied anti-perspirant
I want to inspire, not perspire

My coiffure was the latest style
I had both manicure and pedicure
Brushed my teeth and gargled mouthwash
Don't want bad breath, for sure

I appraised myself in the mirror
Not too bad for an older dame
The occasion, a 3 year old graduation
No need to cause the child shame

One last glance in the mirror
I'm ready to go at last
I leaned over to give the child a kiss
And heard, "O'ma, you gots a mustache!"

Whipping Boy Where Are You?

They said it was for his own good.
I just didn't see how it would,
This beating that they gave.
His good could be his grave.

Stealing just a loaf of bread
Was his only sin.
I thought it had more to do
With the color of his skin.

I was only eight years old
And he almost fourteen.
We two nearly the same in height
But, he was very lean.

I saw pure evil in their eyes
As they beat him with their fists.
I did not know in my little girl heart
Such prejudice exists.

He's broken now a moaning heap
Groveling on the floor.
One "hero" said that's not enough
And kicked him just once more.

Momma grabbed me by my sleeve
Dragging me away.
I never, ever saw him again
And I still wonder until this day.

Oh, whipping boy where are you?

Where Did Innocence Go?

Momma was raised in the Mississippi delta.
She never knew she wasn't supposed to have
a young Negro girl her age as a best friend.

They both were poor and picked cotton.
They both worked cookin and lookin
after their younger brothers and sisters.

They made their own dolls out of corn shucks,
with cob faces painted with charcoal for eyes
and berry stain for mouths.
And the dolls were neither black nor white
but, simply corn color.

Mom's doll was named Gladys
after a beautiful Aunt.
Manzie's was called Willa.
She said someone told her a story once
about a princess named Willamena,
whose Daddy called her Willa.

And innocence was the children's game.
Manzie married and called the delta home.
Momma married and moved to the city, 200 miles away.
Both had babies, momma just one.
Manzie, well, more than one.

The word came down that Momma was sick.
Manzie sent her younger sister to look after her
and care for the husband and child.
Her name was Georgia.
She of the swishy hips and ample bosom.

She hugged me so tight I could hardly breathe.
Even now I am comforted
By remembering her cooing to me,
"I luvs ya, and when I luvs ya, I luvs ya alllll over."

When Momma recovered you returned home.
I was lost without you
to sing to me and threaten
to sweep me out the door,
when I got in the way of your broom.

I remember how scared you were of Gypsies.
How tight you held me,
afraid they would snatch me away
And carry me off because I
Loved their music and dancing.
So, you made up dances of your own
and sang beautiful songs to entertain me.

I loved you Georgia.
You helped form me.
You gave me all the good stuff inside you.
And you helped my Momma get well.
I wish you knew, that she's 89 years old.
I wish I knew, what happened to you.
I wish I could tell you
how important you were to me.

I wish I knew, where
all that innocence went.

A Soldier's Wife

In the gathering darkness they stood
Bodies pressed tightly together
Stars in their eyes as well as the skies
Impervious to the chilling weather.

In the candlelit church they stood
Standing slightly apart
Tears in their eyes and smiling sighs
As they were joined heart to heart.

In the antiseptic green hallway he stood
Gazing through the glass
Watching his son born too soon
Not knowing what would come to pass.

In the chalk smelling room they stood
When their son started first grade
Her bulging tummy again with child
His life he thought heaven made.

In the dirty train station they stood
And waved as he rode away
Duty called him to a foreign land
He knew he could not stay.

In the drizzling cold rain they stood
Stared into the yawning hole
As the flag draped casket was lowered
With his war ravaged body, but, not his soul.

For years by her children's side she stood
She had been their biggest fan
They knew she would truly be happy again
When reunited with her man.

In the warm sunshine her family stood
As this Soldier's Wife was laid to rest
She loved unconditionally for a lifetime
Eulogized for what she did best.

Ontogeny Recapitulates Phylogeny

A simple principal really
One cell divides into two.
Mitosis is the process
By which you become you.

^..^

In the early phylogenetic stage
You could be fish or hog,
Amphibian or Mammal,
Or tail wagging Dog.

<o)))))><

Until you climb the evolutionary path,
Each step remembers it's way,
This palenontological warehouse
Becomes who you are today.

Good Advice; HOE TO GROW

"My good hoe as it bites the ground
revenges my wrongs,
and I have less lust to bite my enemies.

Ralph Waldo Emerson

~~~~~~

HOE TO GROW

I hack and hoe
This weedy row
Grow sweet flowers
Grow
~
It is not sport
Not Spa or Resort
De-stinging the retort
Just grow
~
Smack the ground
Knock weeds down
Dispel the frown
But, grow
~
Hold no grudge
Anger's a drudge
Give love a nudge
Now grow
~
Sing a song
With melody strong
It won't be long
You'll grow
~
Work those plants
Bless those Ants
Disabuse "the can'ts"
Hoe to grow

"Hi Hoe, Hi Hoe, it's off to grow I go"

Every Life is Significant

Mother stood in the driveway
slamming the broom repeatedly against
the cracked, mossy concrete.
I strained to glimpse the object of her fury.
To my horror and dismay lay the female Garter Snake I
had nurtured for many seasons.
Charging out the door, I fell to my knees
and lifted the mother
whose belly squirmed with
the new life she carried.
My garden companion was laid in a honeysuckle thicket
under the twirling fragrant vines that had been her home
for several seasons.

I chose not to put that her through the indignity
of having her belly sliced, allowing the young their
possibility of survival.
Even her friend the cat looked on as the movement
slowed and ceased.
Frequently the cat carried the reptile to my doorstep
placing her there with anxious cries for me to come
appreciate her gift.
On occasions I found her wounded
and out came the peroxide and powdered antibiotic
to be applied along with a prayer for healing.

Now the mourners gathered, one gardener, two children, one cat.
Mother refused to participate saying it could have bitten her.

Fear is a mighty weapon.
Ignorance an even greater one.
I found I could not judge my Mother for a lifetime
of fear ingrained since her childhood
on the bayou of the Mississippi delta,
when farming parents left for the fields
leaving children behind
with warnings to watch out for snakes.

As I prune the creeping Honeysuckle,
I'm acutely aware of the three seasons we shared.
and the need to keep my little
gardening friends
grave pristine.

Author's Comments:

"There are relationships with nature that defy any explanation or known science. I think they are glimpses of what peace is really all about. The old cat is gone now. Mother is confined to assisted care nearing 90 years of age. And there are more than a few of my little insect eating friends alive and thriving under the Honeysuckle thicket, courtesy of their earlier ancestor. Life in the garden is good."

The Drinkin Man

His name was Mudd, a Mississippi man
Farmed all day on his daddy's land.
Ate more dust than he could stand.
At night he was Mississippi Mudd, the drinkin man.

He had more girlfriends than the law allowed.
Kept walkin all day behind that plow.
Suns goin down and it's his turn now
To be Mississipi Mudd, the drinkin man.

He took his drinkin ways to town.
Had too many, acted like a clown.
Got thrown out, landed face down.
It riled Mississippi Mudd, the drinkin man.

By his drinkin ways the die was cast
While drivin his pickup much too fast.
This drinkin night would be his last.
The drinkin man rests in the Mississippi Mud.

Chaney, Schwerner and Goodman

Where does truth lie?
Is it buried in this grave of prejudice?
What was the sin that earned them such
an early and unholy death?
Conscience brought them to this place.
Lack of conscience precipitated their
demise.
Evil abounds and death goes unpunished.
Yet this earthen mound of bones bears
witness to what happened here.
Their cries suffocated in the dirt where
no listening ear could hear.
Freedom Summer of 64 was not free for them.
But, helped make it free for those who
followed.
They went to their graves with their music
still inside them. So said, Oliver Wendall
Holmes.
Now all the world can hear their freedom
song.

The Looking Glass

Fault, Fault, Fault, Fault
Blame, Blame, Blame, Blame
Guilt, Guilt, Guilt, Guilt
Shame, Shame, Shame, Shame

Fingers pointing right and left
Accusations run amok
It's always them, never me
It's their peccadillo, what luck

They are all culpable
There's no onus on me
I'm above reproach
The whole world can see

This house I live in is made of glass
I live entirely alone
It's shattering down on my ass
Ricocheting of stones I've thrown

I never loved my fellow man
I pointed out where they were wrong
They claimed to love me anyway
I asked what made them strong

They said it wasn't by their strength
Everything came from above
They were able to love me
Because they had been so loved.

So, I sit here now in these shards of glass
Recounting hatred seeds I've sown
My home was never one of love
Dear God, I wish I'd known.

Muse

He crawls in bed beside me
Pull the covers to his chin
Snuggles up to my back
And slowly draws me in

We cuddle like cold children
He leaves me little room
We fall asleep this way every night
Like a set of spoons

Sometimes we talk for awhile
Other times he'll simply say
Did I do something cute or stupid
That you wrote about today

At first I thought he didn't like
The poems of him I'm spinning
Then I read him one I wrote
And he just sat there grinning

I'm glad to know that he approves
And didn't blow a fuse
What better compliment could I give
Than calling him my Muse

Morning Song

To my remarkable husband

Morning dawns to whirring hummingbird
wings, seeking Sky Rockets nectar, while tent
sides dip and swell in sunrise breezes.
Tender shafts of light fall softly
on beloved features,
eyes closed in peaceful sleep.
Smells of Pine needles and rain
mingled with pleasant body smells
and low breathing sounds.
Messages sent in warm caresses.
Bodies tangled, souls entwined,
spirits lifted to realms of
Creator planned ecstasy.
Earth moves, life changes, surrender is sweet.
Love flows from untapped basins.
Life begets life.
Loves song forever echoing in the consciousness.
Camping in the Valle Vidal with you.

Come Hell or High Water

The Missouri River, that savage river
which descending from it's mad career
through a vast unknown of barbarism,
poured it's turbid floods
into the bosom of it's gentle sister,
the Mississippi."
Mark Twain
"Life on the Mississippi"

~~~~~~

At the junction of these two great rivers
Even Noah would have been impressed.
It became a sixty mile wide lake
And had yet to reach it's crest.

Now on this forty mile Confluence Flood Plain,
In rich earth where corn and sorghum grow,
Developers want to pave and build.
Wal-Mart's good for the economy, you know.

Ducks and geese use the rivers flyways.
In wetlands they stop to feed.
Out of five million acres only sixty thousand remain.
Another parking lot is just what we need.

Land that was once under water
Will hold stores and car dealerships.
All backed by Federal Flood Insurance.
Won't someone read my lips?

This loss of wetland environment.
The nature they will kill.
Means nothing to money minded developers.
Come "Hell or High water" they're determined to build.

The floods of 93 and 95 ravaged this innocent land.
Augustus Busch lost his house in this flood.
We are strangling our own life force,
Writing our epitaph in the earth's blood.

Fantasy Night Flight

When sea fleugels fly and cry at night,
When moondogs dig in the noonday sun,
When nibletts curl up and swoon in the dew drops,
That's when I'll be thinking of you.

When jitsies twirl in the blue green algae,
When ninops gallop in soft white foam,
When bingleys hover over the stars,
That's when I'll be thinking of you.

So snuggle down in your soft safe bed
And don't you worry your sweet little head.
No matter where you go or what you do,
That's when I'll be thinking of you.

Every Boy Needs A Pet

Poor little soul, little shrunken man
Fly undone and penis in hand
Walks these halls without a care
Hat on his head, thinks he's going somewhere.

Where are you going, people ask
And he proceeds to take them to task.
Anyone can see I'm not dressed for a jog
I'm just headed out walking the dog.

He walks that dog night and day
Because in its house, it will not stay.
Its leash is short and the dog is small.
Look close or you won't see it at all.

Research says the elderly respond to a pet
While it's not housebroken,
He's not through training it yet.
If you've visited the home, surely you've met it.
One word of advice...don't try to pet it.

I Can't Find It!

I can't find it, honey
Is the perpetual call I hear.
It makes no difference what I'm doing
His distress is loud and clear.

It's socks or keys or hair brush
Never in their rightful place.
I always put my hand right on it
While trying to keep a straight face.

How can you look without seeing
When it's right under your nose?
I have important things on my mind
Is the way the conversation goes.

He honestly thinks I hide them
To keep him tied to my side.
Then I can always find it
And injure his manly pride.

But, this is all just a symptom
Of our increasingly busy life.
He says, it's just one more reason
To have an organized wife.

Organization is definitely not
My most admirable feature.
It's the love I feel for this husband of mine
This brilliant but, helpless creature.

Tender Moment of Life

Jeff Scoggins, Tact Squad , Memphis Police Dept.

He's strong and brave
His heart is true
Highly skilled professional
Trained to look after you

On a building with scoped rifle
He's been known to spend his day
When threats to his community
Suddenly come into play

Hazardous materials and explosives
At both he's quite adept
Guarding presidents and prizefighters
Sometimes days since he's slept

Been shared with other nations
To help them train their men
Respected by his peers
Dedicated through thick or thin

Then one day they said, "It's time"
The consequences of a life defined
His old yellow cat must be put to sleep
And we held him as he cried

Gran's White Chenille Bedspread

Softly, slowly up the old creaking stairs
Anticipation oozing from every pore.
Gaining the top to be blinded by it's glare
Glowing, ethereal, light in the room's
Center while color swirls all about me.
I'm unaware transfixed on the whiteness.
Last encounters marks long faded.
No teasing cousins to taunt my desire.
I bore no shame, no secret guilt
So strong was my need for regeneration.
Arms outstretched leaping with all my might
To land solidly in the middle.
There to lie once again a now grown man
Under the ceiling fan in my Gran's
Featherbed with it's soap clean, fresh
Air dried White Chenille spread
This place of my premature birth
And early childhood naps.
Thirty nine years of loving memory
Relegated tomorrow to auctioneers gavel.

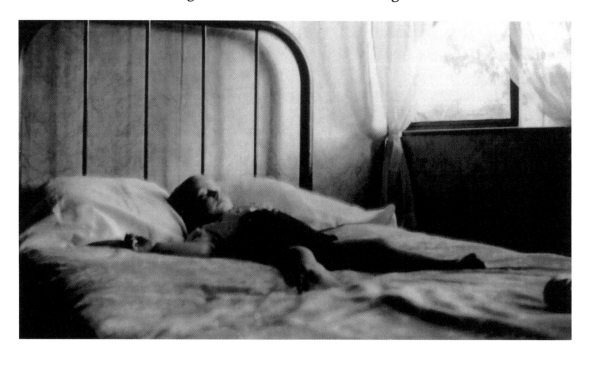

Trolling for Pike

To Ken Broadaway

I drove to my local Bass Pro Shop
To buy a three quarter ounce Erie Dearie
In Halloween colors with forward spinner
For Pike trolling on Lake Erie

<o)))))><

My next stop was at Mike's Bait Shop
For six inch sucker minnows or shiners
If I don't catch fish for our dinner tonight
I'll be eating meatloaf at Rose's Diner.

<o)))))><

I hooked the bait fish through mouth and head
A barb bead so it won't flop free
Look out big fish here I come for you
Don't think you're smarter than me

<o)))))><

Trolling slowly close to the edge of the weeds
The spinner and bait are eighty feet out
I thought it bogged in the vegetation
Then I wanted to shout

<o)))))><

My 6 foot casting rod began to bend
The Pike struck on the forward surge
Twenty pound Fireline was stretched so taut
Reeled quickly, too soon, fight the urge

<o)))))><

I owe my success to Field and Stream
For the right combination of flash, dash and dive
I've just landed my first Northern Pike
Man, It's good to be alive.

<o)))))><

Ken Broadaway catching Peacocks in
the Amazon River, Brazil.

Uncle Hugh (By Gawd)

Hugh Tolleson, Carthage, MS.

His favorite phrase was "By Gawd"
Because that's what he believed.
To everything he laid his hand
Was by God that he achieved.

The land he farmed was given by God.
There was no other truth.
If you dared to disagree
Your name was mud, forsooth.

Livestock all handpicked by God.
He knew them all by name.
Cared for them with loving hand.
Any less would bring him shame.

Under God's watchful eye
He built his family home.
He gathered his children round him
Said this place is on God's loan.

I actually think that he believed
God built his car by hand.
Said if God couldn't build a car
Then, there's no man who can.

His faith was called old fashioned.
God was the center of his universe.
The day he died we laughed and cried
Sure that he thought God had sent his hearse.

Uncle Hugh was as good a man
As ever I have known.
God's own servant tried and true
Now he shares God's home.

I'm sure he's singing hymns of praise
On streets of gold where Angels trod.
And helping everyone he can
With a lot of help "By Gawd."

Pascagoula To Vietnam And Back

Outside the fire hydrant lays down it's life
with the sounds of squealing tires
and crunching gravel.
While the boys out on the edge of the front
porch suck on melting popsicles.
I hear the incoming rounds, drop to my knees,
search for the sanctuary of the dark side
of the refrigerator.

There's rice....I can't ...won't eat rice.
My weapon is gone. I've lost my strength.
Digging with bleeding, bone bared fingers,
my muddy, blood soaked grave.
No mother, no Father, no Wife, no Children
to know where I sent my ghosts spiraling
into the mists of alien atmosphere
and surrendered to mud and rice.

Summoning, who me? Still summoning.
Beige and gold worn linoleum swimming in my
eyes pounded by high top black Converse
tennis shoes.
It's O.K. Dad. Come on Dad. It's O.K.
Hands lifting, patting, pulling me back from
this lingering canker,
putting the demons to bed.

There's water Dad.
Let's go play in the water.

So, we do.

Ron Gordon, a jack of all trades and master of same, now trodding
the boards of most of the community and professional
theatres in Memphis, TN.

Daddy's Dog Sue

The men went to the bottoms to hunt.
Mama wouldn't let me go this time.
I'd hunted with them many times before.
I could handle myself just fine.

She had a list of chores for me to do.
I didn't like being left behind.
I loved the outdoors and being with Dad.
Inside with Mom, I felt confined.

They loaded up the barking dogs.
I heard the tires on the gravel crunch.
Said they'd only hunt an hour or so.
And return in time for lunch.

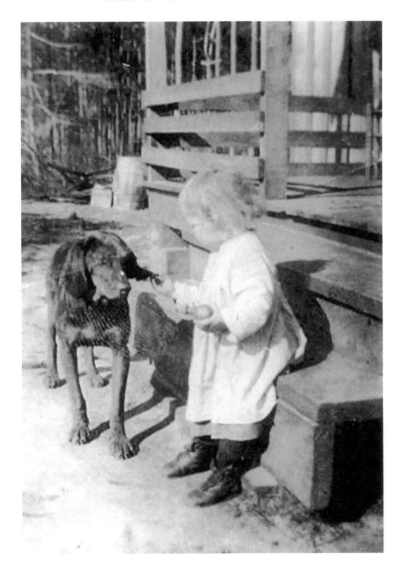

When the lunch time came and went,
They still had not appeared.
Late in the afternoon they arrived
Looking strained and tired and weird.

I ran out to hug my Dad.
He hugged me hard and began to cry.
His friends all stared at the ground
To hide their crying eyes.

I raced around the truck to old Sue's cage.
She was laying on her side.
Jumping a ravine, landed on a staub,
Impaled there she died.

I hugged the dog, howled and cried.
She'd been a little girls friend.
I was mad at Mom who kept me home.
When I could have been with Dad and Sue at ....
The End.

Willie Eugenia (Billie Jean) Conn

Christmas Communion

Matthew Scoggins and Stuart Young, Dec. 24, 2005

Two little boys, friends at the age of 3,
Mysterious to adults or others who see,
Met in the middle of the communion aisle
High fived each other and gave a Christmas smile.

One showed off his bright red shirt.
The other boy, ever alert,
Lifted his sweater to show his new belt.
The children's happiness was what we felt.

They walked the aisle by their parents sides.
Other friends along the way they spied.
This trip was one they did not know.
For them, they thought, it was for show.

Back to their seats they were told to sit,
While deacons saw that all our candles were lit.
The members around us were reduced to tears,
When the boys clicked their candle cups together

And in chorus yelled, "Cheers!"

Before the service we told them of Christ's birth.
And they celebrated his Birthday with 3 year old mirth.
What a gift of joy these little friends bring
To honor their new friend "The Baby King."

Growing Up, But Never Old

Grover Cleveland Conn, Granddaddy

That house never saw paint nor brush
You could spit through cracks in the floor
My heart cries out to see it again
But, alas it is no more

Down the center was an open dogtrot
Large rooms were on either side
Set up on stone pillars just high enough
To provide us great places to hide

The front porch ran the length of the house
Some straight chairs and some that rocked
Off to the right and down a ways
Was the smokehouse Granddaddy kept locked

The front room of the house had a fireplace
Big enough for a man to walk in
Chairs were arranged in the front of it
For the males of my kith and kin

The room also held three old iron beds
Laden with quilts by the pound
If you were lucky enough to sleep in them
You shared them with Granddaddy's hounds

An old bureau stood against one wall
And Great Grandfather's chiming clock
Temperature in the house was extreme to extreme
And the antique finally gave up the "Tock"

In one corner was an old oak washstand
With shaving mirror, pitcher and bowl
It stood in the light from the window
The glass was bubbled and old

By the doorway in the big kitchen
Sat a huge old cast iron stove
The fuel it burned was sticks of wood
The woodbox sat in an alcove

The table itself was ten or twelve feet long
Thrown together from rough hewn planks
The only stool with a back was Granddad's
And he always included a thanks

One Uncle shouted "Pass the bread Morris"
As the blessing ended before Amen was said
The family all laughed and started to eat
As Granddad tossed him his bread

We thirty in number all talked at once
I don't remember just what was said
Maybe hunting dogs, crops and mules, it was
Or the neighbors cow that suddenly dropped dead

Out in the dogtrot stood a wooden icebox
The interior lined with tin
The ice truck came just once a week
And we carried the block ice in

In the rooms across the hall were more iron beds
Feather mattresses and more heavy covers
There was no heat source in this room
So you always slept with others

Under the bed was a porcelain potty
For use at night or inclement weather
If we went to the outhouse after dark
We kids all went together

In winter when it was very, very cold
And you sat on that potty's cold rim
You sat with your cousins staring at you
Your chance of privacy very slim.

In the morning upon awaking
Warmth was your burning desire
You made a mad dash across the cold hall
To stand shivering before the fire

Uncles held quilts while you changed your clothes
Between it and that warm morning blaze
Aunts delivered hot cocoa to us
And warmed our childhood days

I've slept with all my cousins
Many more than just a few
We laughed and fought, kept each other warm
That's what country cousins do

We ran the fields like big wild dogs
Some cousins were really hellions
The only thing that gave us pause
Was finding ripe watermelons

We busted them over our bony knees
Eating our fill with our hands
We knew little of bacteria or other germs
Hygiene came only on demand

We stomped ant hills and robbed hens nests
Carried rabbit tobacco in a poke
Smoking it wrapped in dry corn shucks
And laughed at our dirty jokes

And then one day we all were grown
And later Granddaddy died
The land was sold, house torn down
We cousins held hands and cried

Oh blissful days of childhood
I know you'll never come again
But, Once Upon a Time
There was joy without end

I gaze at these grandchildren of mine
All city born and bred
I tell them stories every day of
Unpainted houses and iron beds

Of a Grandfather with a pet rooster
Flying up and eating off the brim of his hat
And a goat butting us regularly
They say, they wish, they'd seen that

Of days spent helping him shoe his mules
With shoes he made in his shop
And his warnings to us playing near the old well
That always made us stop.

Outhouses, buggy rides and shelling peas
Swatting hornets and dodging snakes
Lots of ghost stories at night by the fire
Sending us to bed with the shakes

Climbing trees and jumping out
Crossing swollen streams on a log
Traipsing long ways through unknown woods
And our only guide was a dog.

So come along children and join me
For the wildest ride of your life
The stories of your O'ma's childhood
Before she became Gim'pa's wife.

1. Royce, Renny, Rita Ann,
and Jimmy Riley Breazeale
Edwin Tolleson
2. Royce, Renny and
Rita Ann Breazeale
3. Carroll Ray, William Stanley,
Linda Kay, Jerry Dale and
Hayden Leroy Thomas
4. Tom and Frank Burkes

56

Dancing With The Shadow

Life was good.
That's how he knew it
Did things he should
And more he shouldn't

Lived it up
Lived it down
Found the meaning
Turned his life around

Days flew by
And so did years
Music flowed
As well as tears

And then one day
Life came apart
The Shadow came
To touch his heart

His eyes looked up
And with a smile
He embraced the shadow
And they danced a while

If he had only been aware
He'd have danced with all his might
For dancing with the Shadow here
Means tomorrow
He'll be dancing with THE LIGHT.

Daddy's Chair Prologue

I was born to a blind father whose character had a profound effect
on my life. He experienced sight problems around nine years of age and
his vision was rapidly going in his teens and totally gone before his twenties.
He was a brilliant man and played five instruments, all self taught. He
opened the first State Office of Rehabilitation in Memphis, TN.
He served under five Presidents. I adored him and early on was convinced
that he had placed the sun, moon and stars in my world. We hunted and
fished together. I helped him with his beautiful woodworking in his
backyard shop. He said I was probably the only five year old around who
knew what a 'bastard file" was. He raised hunting dogs and collected people.

Without sight words framed his existence, both heard, spoken and
sung. He always told me he saw the world through my eyes and wanted
vivid descriptions of things and colors. I developed an extensive vocabulary
at an early age to please him. We had no TV and I read to him. We debated
voraciously. Mother said he'd rather argue with me for 2 hours than agree
with anyone else for 2 minutes. He said I provided him mental stimulation
for the loss of his visual. I disagreed. He had more vision than any sighted
man I knew. He died at 77, of cancer, with grace and dignity in his own bed.
And for a while I was sure God had turned out the lights in my life forever.
I soon came to realize that for a man who never felt defeated or didn't want to be
told that he couldn't do something, my attitude was a slap in his face, not a
homage to his legacy.

He sat in his chair in the evenings of my childhood and I sat leaned back
against his knees while we listened to all the old radio shows. His hand draped
over the side traced the bone structure of my face. He said he knew exactly
how I looked. I never doubted that assertion and it was one of the most
soothing aspects of my growing years. He thought I could do anything and
urged me to try.

Cleaning out Mom's independent living apartment when the need arose
to move to assisted care means getting rid of things with which I'd grown up.
While I adjusted to most of it, it was my Daddy's chair that reduced me to tears
when someone came to look at it. The thought that they could just load it up and
haul it away was almost more than I could bear. To make matters worse, I had
happened on to the last photograph of him sitting in "our" chair. I say our
because I never begrudged him his time in the chair but, anxiously awaited the
time when it was empty. Then I would settle down to read curled up and reassured
of my comfortable position as it's temporary mistress. I was fearless in my
adoration of him and being allowed to share that sacred space with him was a
treasure for me.

Part of its lure was the lingering smell of him that spelled comfort and security to my young mind. I spent many happy hours reading my books in our chair and he always claimed his rent...a vividly described book report.

............it has to go. The grandchildren don't want it because their tastes in furnishing their own homes is a different style. But, they will never find another chair that holds the mystery, the music, the spellbinding drama or the love that this old dusty rose velvet chair holds. I in my stubbornness do not intend to let it go so lightly. Part of the price its future owners will pay is having to listen to the story, its story, my story and ultimately his story. This is not just any chair, you see. How well they listen will probably affect the price. Little do they know that if they love it, I'd gladly give it to them.

Daddy's Chair

TO: The first real man in my life

It was an old rose velvet covered chair.
The back was high, the arms were wide.
He didn't just sit,
He levitated off it's t-cushion.
His turquoise eyes not seeing, yet knowing.
Speaks to me in musical bass
Knowing full well why I sit by his feet.
Caters to my spirit and lifts his bones
Saying, "don't stay up too late now.'
And it's all mine
half sitting, half sprawling,
legs splayed over the arms
I sink lower into the cushiony depths.
Inhaling the scents of tobacco and aftershave
Book in hand
And here in this protected velvet cocoon
I am born and reborn in worlds of dreams.
I capture these word images to share
Enriching his sightless world
As he has enriched mine
Simply by being my Father.

Daddy's Chair Epilogue

Retirement is looming and my husband and I are into the downsizing phase of our life. The chair went to the home of a friend who has lovely antiques. I'm invited to visit it anytime I feel the need. She swears that even after Dad has been deceased 20 years that she can still smell the faint scent of his after shave and cherry pipe tobacco.

The Come Away Train

The notes and chords rattling
around in my brain
are the lonesome sounds
of the come away train.
Waking me from needless slumber,
the lonesome train has my number.
Fall is coming; I need to wander
far afield and over yonder.
For one who's moods
don't ride with rain
I'm tied to fall
and the getaway train.
The mountains are calling,
the fields, the valleys.
I'm leaving behind
these concrete alleys.
Sleeping in caves,
underneath trees,
going to bed and rising
just when I please.
Hitching a ride
to places wild,
vague memories of stories
heard as a child.

Streams of cold water
and stones to cross.
Lunch of fish
on a bed of cool moss.
Reluctant to leave,
I load up my pack
and point myself
back to the tracks.
This wandering time
has fed my need.
Responsibility calls.
Its call I heed.
Maybe next year,
at this very same time,
I'll ride again
on the vagabond line.
With eyes closed now,
I can hear the refrain
of the lonesome sound
of the come away train.

The Architect Is Paraclete

Flushed from safe darkness
Into bewildering light.

Genetically
Replicated
Life form
Documented.

The tabula rasa
Begins its search
For God.

God Chose My Muse

I knew that my love, I'd one day lose.
Then God reached down and chose my muse.
No poems to write, no songs to sing,
Loneliness now a predictable thing.

This vacant feeling in a king size bed.
The scent of the pillow where he lay his head.
No snoring lullaby to help me sleep.
Staring into the dark, too stunned to sleep.

The morning table for coffee and news
Was the favorite place and time, I'd choose.
He'd reach out and pat my hand
And together we made that days plan.

Groceries for me, yard work for him.
Later we tried to work in a swim.
Lunch on the patio under the trees.
Nap in our hammock in the cool breeze.

This was a most rewarding time of life,
For a long time married husband and wife.
Every minute we tried to use,
Until God reached down and chose my muse.

If God needed inspiration he made the right choice.
For over 50 years I delighted at his voice.
Although I will miss him, if I had to choose,
There's no other with whom I'd gladly share my muse.

The Road To Oblivion
(Ode to country roads)

To Attala Co. Mississippi

Where are you goin old black top road,
Windin like a thing possessed
Into torturous hairpin curves,
With your pock marked surface
Like the face of an overly zealous,
Hormoned schoolboy with no place to hide?

I've seen wild hogs stop to drink rain water
Collected in your every pothole and depression
Dogs would come to sniff the rabbits
And possums that lay baking in the sun,
After failing to dodge the wheels
Of a passing car or truck.
The canines rolled on their backs
In the fowl dead smell.
With each passing vehicle,
The vultures flew up to roost
In nearby trees until it was safe
To fly down and resume their meal.

You fed some hungers
You quenched some thirsts.
You took some folks home
To see Mama and Papa and Sis.
You ushered some reckless souls
Into the presence of their God.....
Or not.

Our shoes stuck to your melting surface
In the sun after five days of heat
In the high nineties.

You delivered old women, trained
In birthin babies to the Mama's bedside.
Where children on the other side
Of the bedroom door shivered in fright
At their Mama's screams.

You saw all those cows and hogs
Carried wide-eyed and unknowing
To the slaughter house in trailers
And the backs of pickup trucks.

Men and their dogs traveled on your back
Down into the river bottoms at night
To hunt raccoons and sit on downed logs,
Drinkin strong coffee with floating grounds,
And listen to the music
Of barkin hounds as they ran game
to ground or tree.

You knew the path to the
Monumental Baptist Church
Where country cooks all tried,
At funerals or monthly
dinners on the grounds,
To outdo each other for
The preachers compliments.

Can you count
The big yellow school busses,
with their seats removed,
Piled to their ceilings with
Picked cotton that was
Headed for the gin.

The new four lane super highway
Opened a year ago
With a ribbon cuttin,
And the governor doin the cuttin.
Cars and trucks were lined up for miles
Just so they could say they'd
been the first to use it,
And drive sixty five miles an hour.

Here you sit with the trees
Growin closer to you every day.
And that thick green blanket of Kudzu
Coverin you to reach the other side.
Only a few remember
That you're even here.

So where you goin now
You old worn out used up
Black top road?

I heard it's oblivion.
Someday someone walkin
In these woods
Will stumble up on you
And say to themselves,
"Well, lookie here.
I wonder where this ol' road went?"

But, we know, don't we?

The Waiting Room

This isn't what I wanted to do
Stare at the gum on a strangers shoe.
Birds sing, trees bud, flowers in bloom
While I sit in this Doctors waiting room.

I came prepared to stay a while.
I searched the room for a friendly smile.
I saw one beam from under purple hair
Crippling Arthritis no cause for despair.

I nodded and spoke and tried not to stare
As she smiled and patted the adjacent chair.
I picked up my book and moved to her side.
Her genuine delight was hard to hide.

I listened to stories of love and life
Traveling the world as a gentleman's wife.
Her mind was sharp, her wit was keen.
The others watched our unfolding scene.

She rose and hobbled to the nurses call.
We watched her go, one and all.
For weeks I moaned of aches and pain
Now, I can't remember why I came.

Insults Worthy of Shakespeare

She was a yeasty, weatherbitten strumpet
When she plucked his heartstrings
He a roguish, rough-hewn ratsbane
Was flattered by her attentions

He became a mewling, milk-livered miscreant
In her manipulative hands
Her mother, a frothy, flap-mouthed fustilarian
Moved in, much to his dismay

He told the churlish, common-kissing codpiece
To leave and she laughingly refused
She and her mammering, motley-minded mammet
Said he was their prisoner forevermore

The Moral of The Story:
When a strumpet plucks your heartstrings and
immediately says,"I want you to meet my
mother." It's time to pick up your puny,
puking, pox-marked, pignut puttock and
head for the hills.

"It is my contention that a poem can be construed in such a way
that it is quite understandable to the reader although they don't know
the meaning of all the words. I guess you'd call it reading between the lines."

Two of Memphis theatres finest actors
Ann Marie Hall, in a past production at
the University of Memphis,
and George Dudley, in a production of "Kiss Me Kate,"
done in Fort Atkinson, WI. in 1989. George adds, "with
hair and everything."

Limericks 1 & 2

Blue Blood

There was a young man from Yazoo
Whose blood was terrifically blue
His nose so turned up
It looked like a cup
And he drowned in a heavy dew.

Mr. NoS mo king

A dumb young lad, Ebeneezer
Through smoking became quite a wheezer
He coughed and he hacked
By Emphysema was attacked
Didn't live to become an old geezer

Limericks 3, 4, & 5

What Lies Beneath

A dapper dan named Ben Lesser
Was known as quite a dresser
His rear white as snow
Skinny-dipping did show
Would he do it again? Replied "yessir."

Working Girl

Her flirtatious ways were well known
For in this town she'd grown
No man was safe
From this sexy waif
Until the town she did own

Two Views

Two children out to play
Found a dirty picture they say
One went to repent
One to Hollywood went
Priest and Producer, still friends today.

Limericks 6, 7 & 8

Young Girl from Nantucket

There was a young girl from Nantucket
Who shlept milk to market in a bucket
Bought a truck called Ford
Her cows said, "Good Lord"
Now all she has to do is "truckit"

Lad From Westminister

There was a young lad from Westminister
Whose ways were rather sinister
He prowled at night
Giving towns folks a bite
Kept the whole countryside, in a stir

Nosy Rosy

There was a young lass named Rose
Who had a short button nose
Though she didn't pick it
She did tend to stick it
Where a proboscis never goes.

My Life In a Plastic Garbage Bag

A New Orleans Survivor

What's in your plastic Garbage bag?
My life, only my life.
Marriage license, birth certificates and photos
Of my beloved wife.

I held on to her as long as I could.
She said, "Let go, let go,
Save the children," then was washed away
Photos all I have to show.

One child on my shoulders, one on each arm
We began to kick and swim.
Another's child came floating by.
I reached out for him.

He grabbed me hard around the neck.
I thought I'd surely drown.
Then my feet struck something hard.
I had touched the ground.

We're waiting now in this sheltered place,
A family put together.
One was lost and one was gained
By Katrina's nasty weather.

These children and I owe our lives
To this one selfless heart.
And this plastic garbage bag and I
Will never be apart.

New Orleans

They all fall down,
the stars,
the stars.

The light shown around,
the moon,
the moon.

Where is the ground?
Under water,
under water.

What is that sound?
The wind,
the wind.

Boats came round,
escape,
escape.

Replaced my frown,
I'm alive,
I'm alive.

City of renown,
all gone,
all gone.

The Story of Our House

To the children in my childhood home

To minds eye it remains a mansion
Set in trees, high upon a hill
Playful rainy afternoons on a screened in porch
Roamed the neighborhood at will

In backyard trees of apple or peach
Writing poetry with pencil and paper
Registering my kingdom beneath the trees
Seeking no adult favor

The only girl on a street of boys
Made games of rock and sticks and seeds
Played unobserved in woodland stream
Sprouted tall and strong like a healthy weed

Yesterday I returned to view
That mansion on the hill
Two bedroom house just a postage stamp
I stared without goodwill

I took that hill, now just a bank
In two long steps
The porch only three by five
No fruit trees had been kept

I wandered down to my friendly stream
To soothe this nervous itch
Once again I stood aghast
It's a deep concrete drainage ditch

I met the family living there
They were of a different race
I shared all my memories with them
They knew I'd loved that place

The children now stay close to home
It's not the safest place to live
They loved the stories of their house
Asked if I had more to give

Those children sat at my feet
With eyes so big and wide
They traveled back to a fairy land
And I was their fairy guide

They saw their house and neighborhood
Through my eyes dimming with time
And vowed to write their story down
And merge it into mine

Today the postman delivered
A large manila envelope.
Inside I saw "The Story of Our House"
And it's everything I'd hoped.

Fifteen Minutes of Infamy

His fifteen minutes of "fame"
Was achieved in a unique way.
The reason was pretty lame
But, it saved his life that day.

He went duck hunting in the Bayou
Got his limit and was feeling great.
A glance at his watch showed two
Now, he took measure of his fate.

He and Lab, Josie, headed back.
He'd left his jacket in the boat.
They waded around for hours
In that watery waist deep moat.

The sun went down, sky turned black
He ate a raw duck breast
He'd left his buddies by a train track
He knew they were doing their best.

Man and Lab sat down on a log.
Helicopters soon were in the sky,
Camouflage clothes and big black dog,
And the copters passed them by.

They'd been missing for twelve hours.
He was cold and tired and wet.
He fantasized about hot showers
And getting Josie to the Vet.

A sudden sound alerted him
And then he had a thought.
Under waders and hunting pants
Was neon underwear his wife bought.

On the barrel of Benelli Super Back Eagle
He waved his neon flag.
The copter lit him in a bright spotlight
And Josie's tail began to wag.

He has made all the papers
What a great story to tell.
How wife and chartreuse underwear saved his life
Cause when she'd bought it, he gave her "Hell."

You Can Go To...............(The Cottage)

I begged and begged until he honored my pleas
And built me a cottage out in the trees
Insulated and paneled with old beadboard
With left over, broken tile, it was floored

Lots of windows to let in the light
Two lamps and a chandelier for use at night
An old wicker rocker so I might rest
Framed family pictures that I love the best

A handmade pine wardrobe holds all my tools
For grandchildren and me, there are no rules
It's their hide-away for rest or play
It's a place where I can write all day

There's a potting bench for work with flowers
And what seems like minutes turns into hours
There's books, an easel, and music, and more
I automatically relax when I pass through the door

And old Hoosier cabinet makes a great display
And a shelved shoe rack that rolls out of the way
The path through the trees is lined with flowers
The smell is heaven after soft Summer showers

He tells me now if he'd only known
The calming effect on me it's shown
It would have been built forty years or so
Then he could have told me "Where to go."

"Lingering Sea-Fever"

{I must down to the seas again, to the lonely sea and the sky,
And all I ask is a tall ship and a star to steer her by,
And the wheel's kick and the wind's song and the white sail's shaking,
And a grey mist on the sea's face, and a grey dawn breaking.}

They sit by the shore, man and dog
longing for the adventure of the sea.
The animal bred through many generations
to ride the ships of the North Atlantic,
out of Newfoundland, rescuing
unfortunate sailors who fall overboard.

{I must down to the seas again, for the call of the running tide
Is a wild call and a clear call that may not be denied;
And all I ask is a windy day with the white clouds flying,
And the flung spray and the blown spume, and the sea-gulls crying.}

Her life has been one of luxury
in the loving laps of little blond girls.
Never experiencing the work genetically planned
for her but, always yearning for the water.
Now nearing the culmination of her
dog years.
The man in mid-life
after years of work and study
preparing him for high powered existence
in corporate America, finds himself
Slowing and changing direction.

{I must down to the seas again, to the vagrant gypsy life,
To the gull's way and the whale's way where the wind's like a whetted knife;
And all I ask is a merry yarn from a laughing fellow-rover
And quiet sleep and a sweet dream when the long trick's over.}

He and the dog come now frequently to the sea
and sit, each in a world of their own creation,
Yet more closely aligned than
either would guess.

Adapted from: "Sea-Fever"
By John Masefield (1878-1967).(English Poet Laureate, 1930-1967.)

Frederick Cossitt (Rick) Stanford and Newfoundland
"Kimber" on the beach at Pawley's Island.

Little Girl Dreams

For my 4 Granddaughters

Windows raised,
Scents of honey suckle and mock orange
Screens plastered with cottonwood pollen
Drawn in by the squeaking attic fan in the hall

Outside friends who don't take naps
Continue their play in the noonday sun
While I slowly sink into realms of dreams
Staring at the framed lone wolf picture on the wall

My cannonball four poster bed is my faithful steed
I ride like the wind over the hills of the wolf
Rattlesnake engorged with rabbit eyes me suspiciously
Sun bakes my skin and streaks my hair

My mountain path is rim rocked by recent rains
I know no fear plunging down the mountainside
Horse is stumbling, body tumbling, searching, grasping
I lay crumpled in a narrow ravine barely alive

The sound of a footstep and then another
Face being washed lavishly by a dog's tongue
Eyes open to see the cowboy leaning over me
He gently lifts me onto his horse and flicks the rein

For days I live in a fragmented dream until
I awake with him sitting beside me, my dream come true
My name is Roy Rogers and this is my dog Bullet
After Dale left me, I swore I'd never love again

Then there you were the girl of my dreams
Dropped out of the heavens for me to care for
Will you marry me and ride the Silver Sage by my side
My horse Trigger is waiting outside to carry us away.

Yes, Yes, I say, I've waited for you for so long
I watch you every Saturday at the Paramount
Saving lives and locking up the bad men.
I've seen every movie you've ever made

He leans in to kiss me with eyes closed
Bad breath jolts me awake to find my red Dachshund
Sniffing my face and staring intently into my eyes
Hers saying, I'm awake now, play with me

So much for the dreams of a little girl
Who lived in books and weekend movies
Who never resented taking naps
And went to sleep in the bosom of flower smells

Whose grandest treat was afternoon visits by the Popsicle man
Or sitting on the floor by the Philco floor model radio
Listening to the radio shows with Daddy
His seeing eye dog curled around his feet

I'll always have honeysuckle and mock orange in my yard
Along with lilacs and roses and maybe a gardenia
To cherish the sweet fragrance of my Southern girlhood
To remind me of riding into the sunset with Roy Rogers

Legacy

The sun has yet to grace this place.
I'm peeling back the layers of sound.
I come to my favorite writing place,
Spread my blanket on the ground.

This earth the fount of all that is seminal
Bringing a new level of perception.
The essence of this life is spiritual
Recharging life force with earthly meditation.

I'll shake off my worldly preoccupation
And sense the pulse of the universe.
I am privileged beyond imagination
To fill this void with my verse.

A cacophony of birds sings observance
Of cosmic divisions between dark and light.
The sun slowly makes it's entrance
Shaking off it's armor of night.

I write of testimony and reflection,
Of life as a passing parade.
Each marching in our own direction
Unaware of the impression we've made.

This life is the boat I was given
And no matter if I sail near or far.
Each day is worth the living
As I guide it by my own star.

I search for the quintessential expression
To explain life's innate potential.
To live with passion and compassion,
Integrity is never inconsequential.

How will history regard me?
I have no way to tell.
I leave these writings so all can see
They knew me very well.

I've given everything I have to give
Of love and faithfulness too.
I cannot tell you how to live
Except, to yourself be true.

Someday if you find my writing place
And spread your blanket on the ground,
Sharing warm earth and sun on your face
You'll sense my spirit still around.

A Toast

To will,
to wit,
to want,
to die,
To drain the glass and lift it high.
To sift the dust of a life lived right.
To search for God in the still dark night.

To loss,
to despair,
to tears,
to need,
To books I've read and yet to read.
To children fed from meager stores.
To strangers washed from foreign shores.

To love,
to laughter,
to run,
to dance,
To time now ending, take your chance.
How you do it is your call.
The young will rise as elders fall.

My parents shared a beautiful love story for 50 years. I've often wondered how they felt about their life. I write so that my children and grandchildren won't have to wonder about mine. This collection has been a labor of love. We rarely appreciate the intrinsic value of our growing up experiences until years later. What seems to be trivial and mundane takes on beautiful proportions when viewed from the vantage point of age. We are destined to learn more from a memory of an event, than the actual incident. If there is one thing to teach our children, it is live in the moment, savor each event as if it's the most important that will ever happen to them, whether viewed as good or bad. The impact of these events help make us who we are. I am *Madalyn McKnight Stanford*, child of God and daughter of Byron Burton (Bob) McKnight & Mary Kathleen Conn McKnight. And by the way, it helps to laugh a lot!

About the Author

Madalyn is a 65-year-old retiree, wife of a practicing Pediatrician, mother and grandmother. She started reading and writing at 5 and says, "It's amazing what you can do growing up without television." She resides in Memphis, TN. with husband Jim and shares his love of travel.

She was born a privileged, underprivileged child of a blind father and family with meager monetary support and over abundant resources.

Can't was a forbidden word in her home. A happy, enthusiastic, talented musician father was a people magnet and made life fun. Her mother kept them clean, fed and all together, allowing for the fun. She had parents who adored each other and shared that adoration with the children.

Her husband, as she describes him, is a man of great humor and compassion who has allowed her the freedom to try her wings at anything she fancied. She raised a large active family in the city of her birth. The place where in the 40s and 50s, they went to the same schools, churches and shopped at the same 5 and 10 cent stores. She has faced the familial breast cancer of the maternal side of her family and remains in awe of her mothers' 90 year life span while losing her sister at 45. Grandchildren energize her. Always adventurous, she spent the summer of 1994 living in a tent she called her "Canvas Chateau" in the mountains of New Mexico leading groups hiking up into the high ranges.

No longer able to backpack and climb, she has returned to writing and the stage, acting and working behind the scenes of community theatres and volunteers for numerous organizations from the arts to inner city families.

Printed in the United States
66878LVS00001B